In Wineseller's Street

For Wilson,

Drink up! Some great
"wine" (love) from Iran.

Enjoy!

2001

Also by Thomas Rain Crowe

Poetry

Learning To Dance
Poems For Che Guevara's Dream
Deep Language
The Personified Street
New Native
Water From The Moon
The Laugharne Poems

Translations

Why I Am A Monster (Hughes-Alain Dal)
10,000 Dawns (The Love Poems of Yvan & Claire Goll)

Essays

You Must Go Home Again
The Perfect Work

Anthologies

A Celtic Resurgence: The New Celtic Poetry
(Poets from Scotland, Ireland, Wales, Brittany,
Cornwall and the Isle of Man)

In Wineseller's Street

Renderings of Háfez by
Thomas Rain Crowe

Ibex Publishers

In Wineseller's Street
Renderings of Háfez by Thomas Rain Crowe

Copyright © 1998 by Thomas Rain Crowe

Some of the poems in this volume have previously appeared in *Oxygen* (#13, 1995; #15, 1996), and *Nexus* (Fall, 1994)

Illustrations are by Ali Dowlatshahi and are from *Persian Designs and Motifs for Artists and Craftsmen* published by Dover Publications Inc., New York, 1979.

Cover drawing by David Roberts, 1839

Manufactured in the United States of America

ISBN 0-936347-67-8

The paper used in this book meets the minimum requirements of the American National Standard for Information Services - Permanence of Paper for Printed Library Materials, ANSI Z39.48-1984

Ibex Publishers
8014 Old Georgetown Road
Bethesda, Maryland 20814
Telephone: 301-718-8188
Facsimile: 301-907-8707
Internet: www.ibexpub.com

Library of Congress Cataloging-in-Publication Information

Háfiz, 14th cent.
[Divān. English. Selections]
In wineseller's street : renderings of Háfez / by Thomas Rain Crowe.
p.   cm.
ISBN 0-936347-67-8
I. Crowe, Thomas Rain.   II. Title.
PK6465.Z31C76   1998
891' .5511--dc21   97-43461
CIP

for Christopher,
sun & son

Preface

Sufism, during the early part of this millennium, has given the world not only a universalist spiritual tradition, but a poetic tradition much overlooked referred to as "the path of love." Handed down orally for generations, then eventually transcribed into print, the poetry of the Perfect Masters (complete, God-realized souls) of this primarily oral tradition falls into the hands of late twentieth century translators and poet/versionists just in the nick of time, when it is needed most.

The poems of Khwaja Shamseddin Mohammad Háfez, known in the West simply as Háfez, were composed during the fourteenth century in Persia, amidst a time of much political and religious upheaval. Consequently, the poetry of Háfez reflects these turbulent times in imagistic detail. Following in the footsteps of Jalaleddin Rumi, whom most would consider the creator of the Sufi mystic poetic tradition and who was a Perfect Master who lived a century earlier during the thirteenth century, Háfez continues the "path of love" poetic tradition through his own century, leaving his legacy for such mystic Sufi poets as Yunus Emre and then, in the fifteenth century, Kabir. From these four poets, alone, there is established an early literary tradition of hope, love, and universal harmony much in opposition to the Western literary tradition which came out of Europe during the second half of the millennium, mirroring the confusion, imbalances, loss of spiritual connectedness, and ennui brought on by the Industrial Revolution and global capitalism.

Much celebrated in his own day, Háfez was in much demand, and active in courts throughout the Middle East. Said to have received his poetic gifts from the prophet Elijah who gave him a drink of the waters-of-life, Háfez, like Rumi before him, traveled around Persia reciting his poems which were written down by his students and scribes.

In much the same spirit as the Welsh "Praise" tradition, the Sufi dervish tradition emphasizes the spiritual values of hopeful reverence, thanksgiving, unification and joy. Done in an oral stylistic form, and very much dedicated to the ear of the listener, the "ecstatic" poems, as they are referred to today, of Háfez and his perfect comrades, use symbolism and stylistic imagery and metaphor to carry the weight of their subject matter. Chief among these recurring symbolic images, along with others such as "the rose," "garden," "ocean," "the door," "pearl" and various endearing names for God, is the metaphor of "wine." It is precisely around this metaphor that this collection of Háfez's poetry is centered.

Taken from Háfez's complete collection of poems, the *Divan*, I have selected some seventy-four poems dealing with or orbiting around the subject of "wine." In this context the principal metaphor of wine is addressed as the "Winebringer," "Winekeeper," "Winehouse," and "Winestreet." And it is from these references that I have selected "Winestreet" as the title for this book. For in these poems, everything happens in Winestreet – the street of the Divine. It is here that God, the Wineseller, lives, who is the source of all of Háfez's suffering and spiritually romantic longing. His place of refuge is the Winehouse, where he drowns his sorrows in the blood of the Beloved, red wine.

Sounding much like such poets as Han Shan of the Chinese Buddhist "wine-drinking" tradition, Háfez, much like his contemporary Yunus Emre (who is called "the greatest folk poet in Islam"), brings poetry out of the courts and throne rooms of the East and into the streets. His imagery and poetic rhythm are direct and written for the common man. In my versioning of these poems from the *Divan* from more literal and academic translations done earlier this century, I have tried to be true to the "folk" and/or peasant sensibilities which I believe to be inherent in the original Persian. Like the Welsh-Language poets of the European peasant "Praise" tradition, these poems, not unlike Shakespeare's plays, are written for the common man in common everyday speech. It is in this spirit that I have done these American versions. Bringing into the late twentieth century American dialect the inflections, idioms, and sensibilities that, I believe, reflect what would be the voice of Háfez were he to appear, suddenly, in Chicago, New York, Atlanta or Los Angeles reciting his poems from out of the gyre of his Sufi dervish dance.

In Wineseller's Street is a book of poems about hope. About a world seen through eyes that don't idolize individualism and separation. It reflects the human potential of living in a world of harmony and grace. No poet, and no tradition does this better than Háfez and his Sufi friends. During a time of international political and religious chaos and violence, perhaps no other work is more essential to our survival and recovery. Here, Háfez is accessible, and in his accessibility, concise. Always the humble teacher, Háfez the Perfect Master sits with us on the barstool in the town pub like a mirror, reflecting back our dreams....

— Thomas Rain Crowe

— 1 —

Hey, Winebringer, fill our cups with the light of wine!
Hey, minstrel, sing us our favorite song!

The face of the Beloved is reflected from this cup of wine.
You fools, you don't know what you're missing!

Dancing and flirting all night in the bar is good fun,
Until the Ancient One walks through the door dancing like
the branches of a pine.

He is the one whose heart is alive with love, and will never die:
The history of the world is full of writing about ourselves as if
we were He.

On Resurrection Day, the lawful bread of the priests
Will be no better than this outlaw's wine.

O wind, if you are going past the rosebed of the Beloved,
Please take this message:

"Why have you taken our names from Your memory book?
Now, our names will be out of sight."

Winter is coming, and like the tulip my heart is closing from the cold:
O Bird of Paradise, when will you come again to our cage?

In the eyes of the Beloved that have stolen our hearts is the best drink!
And we are drunk, like a horse is slave to the farmer's reins.

In the blue-green sea of sky, the crescent moon floats like a boat,
Yet is drowned in the gaze of the Beloved.

Háfez, keep on dropping the grain of tears from your eyes,
It could be the Bird of Union that takes our bait one night!

—2—

O pilgrim, come and look into the mirror of this glass of wine!

Pick up your net, the Pure Bird can never be caught.
There is nothing in this cage but wind.

Live for the moment! When the water in the lake dried up
Even Adam left the Garden of Safe Joy.

At the Mardi Gras of Life, have one or two cups of wine, then leave.
Don't hang around waiting for an enlightened drunk!

Say to your heart: "My youth is gone."
Even though you have picked no roses, use your old head skillfully,
then do the right thing.

The puritan know-it-all never sees the drunkard
Or secrets hidden behind the veil.

O Wise One, those of us who sit all day on Your threshold have more than
Earned our pay. For service rendered,
to pay Your slaves in pity is o.k.

When I handed the reins of my heart to You,
I gave up forever any hope of becoming anything other than a horse.

O student of the cup of Háfez; drink and then go like the wind
To the Master and tell him the story of this great wine!

— *3* —

Wake up Winebringer! And pour me a glass of wine.
Throw dust on the head of this sad earth man.

I've taken off my snazzy blue coat and bare-chested
I clutch this full cup.

Even though the rich or the politicians call us "trash,"
To us their blue blood or fame means nothing.

Give me more wine! All their dust blowing around in the wind of pride
And desire is as worthless as a hole.

The smoke from my burning heart
Gags all those with ignorance as their goal.

My mad heart has a secret
That no one knows.

The Beloved has stolen even the sweet solitude from my heart,
And I am content.

No one who has ever laid eyes on this silver-limbed Cypress,
Would ever go looking in the woods for a cypress again.

"Háfez," the voice of inner wine will say;
"Be careful what you ask for, you may just get what you want!"

— 4 —

The rose speaks to the nightingale and says:
"It is time again for Youth to come into the garden."

O wind, take this message to children playing in the fields,
To the cypress, basil and the rose.

And if the Wineseller's apprentice is an admirable child,
I will sweep the dust from the Winehouse door with my eyelashes.

O moonsweep, don't brush my mind clean of this ecstasy!

Those that turn their noses up at drunkards in the name of religion
In the end will end up in the same place.

Best to befriend a Man of God, for even in Noah's Ark
Not even the humble dust was turned to mud as the water rose.

Instead, say to the man who sleeps in the street at night:
"What use are skyscrapers, that reach up to touch the sky?

"Let's leave this earth-house and stop living by bread alone.
This meal without wine is worse than death."

O man of Canaan, the throne of Egypt is yours!
It's time to say good-bye to this prison.

Time to let down your musky hair!

For not even a word of the Secrets of Being will you understand,
Looking only into the eyes of what is possible.

Freedom and contentment are treasures
That the Sultan or the King will never own.

Háfez says; "Don't make the Koran a trap for ignorance.
Go out and drink wine. Get drunk and be happy and laugh
at those who live in this cage."

Winebringer, bring that expensive wine you've been saving, for the
President of the World Bank or all the sheik's land will not be found
in Paradise!

If a holy man would take this heart in His hand,
For that man's birth-mole I'd trade England and Thailand, too.

The beautiful face of the Beloved doesn't need
Makeup, eyeliner, perfume or our imperfect love.

I know for a fact that the beauty of Joseph, growing daily,
Brought out from behind the veil the beauty of Mary, too.

People have always called me names, and now I am happy.
God bless them, for a bitter name is sweet from a ruby lip painted with
too much rouge.

O young people, listen to this good advice: Cherish the teachings
Of the wise old Masters even more than the voice of your heart.

Let's drink good wine and sing great songs instead of talking about Destiny.
Reason can't fit into that full glass, or between the notes of that song.

Listening to this ghazal of Háfez is like stringing pearls; sing it sweetly,
And wear that song like stars!

— *6* —

Summer breeze, go gently to the graceful gazelle and say:
"Why have you sent us away to deserts and mountains?"

O seller of such sweet sugar, whose life will always be long,
Why not ask about the parrot who needs sugar all day?

When you sit there with the Beloved drinking fine wine,
Think of us lovers drinking the wind of hard luck.

Hey rose, perhaps pride in Your own beauty has stopped Your heart
From asking about the sobbing of the sad nightingale.

Wise birds are not fooled by deceit and clever cages,
It is kindness and real beauty catch men who see the truth.

Dark-eyed and moon-faced, I can't say why
It is that such deceit exists.

This much I can say for sure: Your beauty is flawless,
And it's a shame You keep loyalty and devotion such a secret.

Think of all those who wander lost in deserts and fields,
And give thanks to good fortune and good friends.

It's no wonder that the poems of Háfez would cause
The Messiah to dance. These are wonderful songs, and Venus sings!

Where am I without recognition, where is work's reward: where?
Look at this long path, where does it end: where?

Where is the link between drunkenness and pious virtue?
Where is the lute's melody, the preacher's loud voice: where?

I am sick and tired of this religious cell and this monk's clothing;
Where is Wineseller's Street, and the taste of pure wine: where?

O Beloved, where have You gone?
Where is that glance, that condemnation: where?
May our reunion be a sweet memory!

What do dark hearts and hate have to gain from Your face?
Where is the quiet lamp or the candle of the sun's radiation: where?

The dirt and dust from Your threshold is the source of balm for my eyes;
Is there anywhere else but here? Where else can I go: where?

The dimple on my chin is nothing more than a pit:
O heart, where are you going in such a rush: where?

O friend, do not look at Háfez for sympathy and an easy life;
He will only ask you where you are from, and where you are going: where?

— *8* —

Winebringer, bring me some wine to expand my heart and make it forever new.
Singer, sing me a sweet song, forever fresh and new!

With the Beloved dressed in finery, come and sit for a while.
And from these lips sip the kiss of longing, forever fresh and new.

Winebringer! More wine!
Keep my glass full, forever fresh and new.

When will you ever enjoy the fruit-of-life if you don't drink wine?
A toast to the Beloved! forever fresh and new.

Look how that pretty girl is coming on to me,
In tight clothes, perfume, and all that rouge, forever fresh and new.

O morning breeze, when you blow over the Beloved's street,
Tell the story of Háfez's love, and make it forever fresh and new!

— *9* —

O Beloved, since Your good looks have seduced me into loving You,
Both heart and soul have fallen into ruin, from head to foot.

Being separated from You Your true lovers endure.
Those who know this longing are only the thirsty and the few.

O my soul, if my Beloved is consumed with loving and drunkenness,
Then I am going to give up piety, and soberness too!

The time of pleasure and joy is the season of wine:
Think of it as war, and the spoils of a work-week awarded to you.

Háfez, if it helps you to kiss the foot of the Beloved, then do it.
Both worlds are waiting for you: the world invisible and the world of grace!

Morning comes veiled in thin clouds.
Friends, sing "morning cup, morning cup" out loud!

As dew runs down the face of the tulip,
My friends, to drink wine, have vowed!

From the fields where the breeze of Paradise blows,
Drink, forever, that wine.

In the field, the rose has placed its emerald throne;
"Go get me wine that's as red as a ruby," I say.

The Winehouse door is locked.
"Open the door, Wineseller!" I cry.

Why would they close the Winehouse
In the face of thirsty travelers?

This is like pouring salt
On a wounded heart, and laughing.

O fanatics and pious wise ones,
Guzzle your wine and pray!

If you are looking for the Fountain of Youth,
Gaze into your wineglass, and listen for the sound of the harp.

Like Alexander the Great, know that if you are searching for Life,
The Beloved's red ruby lip is life's cloud and life's rain.

Just as the face of the Winebringer is promise of more wine,
Promise to drink wine in rose season.

Háfez, do not worry and grieve; at the end of the wedding the Bride of
Fortune will lift her veil, and you can look into her shining face!

Being in the garden of Union with You is like being in the garden of Paradise.
But the pain of this separation from You is like living in the heat of Hell's fires.

Still, I have been living in the beautiful branches of Your tree
Like a bird of paradise, sheltered from the storm.

All night long I look down at Paradise Creek
And it's like looking at You eye to eye.

The chapter on the season of Spring describes, perfectly, Your beauty:
Each book I read mentions Your grace.

Even though my soul hasn't caught up with my heart's desire, my heart is consumed.
If I had achieved my dream, would blood be spilling from these eyes?

Many are there who, with wounded hearts and livers,
Suffer the sting of salt from Your lips.

And not only believers are drunk on Your love;
Listen to the mad griefstricken wails of a million fanatics!

In Your face, I see the ruby-red shine of the sun,
Which brightens both world and sky.

Pull up the veil! How long will You keep us in such suspense?
Except for Your privacy, what purpose does this closed door serve?

The rose has seen Your face, and it burst into flames!
From Your fragrance alone, shame has become the rosewater of desire.

In love with Your face, Háfez is drowning in this sea of desire.
Look at him there floundering in the waves. Come and help him before he dies.

Háfez, don't be stupid. Don't let life pass you by
Without understanding what this life means.

— 12 —

This house in my eye is Your home.
Enter with respect and with an open heart.

Your face steals the hearts of spiritual seekers.
Captured with the bait of grain and charm.

Listen to the nightingale! How happy it is united with the rose.
Its loving song can be heard only while walking in Your field.

O Beloved, cure our sick hearts with Your healing kiss.
Heal us with a dose of Your wine

Even in service, my body is unworthy of You;
And my soul, merely dust on your doorstep.

What a horseman You are!
So good that a wild colt obeys You with the mere sight of the whip.

You want to know what I think when
Even the juggling sky is overwhelmed by the tricks of Your game?

Here is what I think: The music of Your party is loud and
Goes on all night long. The poems of Háfez are only two notes in that tune.

— *13* —

In the old days when I was drunk, the wish for reverence and discipline
Was all far away. I was well-known for drinking too much wine on the
birthday of the Big Bang.

Then, every time I performed "Hail Mary's" in the fountain of Love,
Four times after that I'd chant "God is great!"

Give me some more wine, so I can recite to you the poem of the Mystery of Fate.
Whose face is my lover and from Whose bouquet I am drunk again today.

From where I sit, the waist of a mountain is smaller than the waist of an ant.
I am a worshipper of wine, and can still see the welcome door.

O that I may stay in this state of drunkenness to fend off any evil eye!
Underneath this blue sky no one lives or stays happy forever–

In vision's garden, no rosebud is sweeter than the rosebud made by the Creator.
If I am lying, may my soul be ransom for His kiss.

Because He and you are One, like the spray is part of the ocean wind,
Háfez became a Solomon to show you that kind of love.

— *14* —

The bigot who flaunts his reverence, knows Nothing of knowledge.
Whatever he may say about us, there is no reason to be concerned.

When on the Path, whatever happens to a pilgrim is for his own good.
The heart is not lost in the bends of that straight road.

So that you can see how the fame changes, I will move a pawn.
On a chessboard of drunken lovers, there is no checkmate.

What is this high smooth roof I see with so many pictures?
In this world, if you know the answer to this mystery, you are no great sage.

O Lord, what is this freedom, this powerful force:
Where there are hidden wounds but no strength left to talk.

I suppose you could say, "the Lord of Secretaries doesn't know the account."
And "His Royal Signature knows no date."

Say: "Come," to who wants to come, "Speak" to who is tired of silence.
In this courtroom there is no arrogance, and no stern doorman at the gate.

The only one here out of shape is the one who is form-less:
It is not the cloth that has been cut too large.

Only those with pure hearts go straight to the Winehouse door;
For these, entry to Wineseller Street is free.

I am a slave of the Perfect Master, whose gift, like wine, constantly flows;
Unlike the priest and the bigot who are never late.

If Háfez is not sitting in the highest seat in any room, it's because of
His elevated spirit. True Lover, you who drink only the dregs of this great
wine, know you are not trapped by wealth and money, and are free!

— 15 —

The messenger who came from the land of the Master,
Brought my life's destiny, written in His hand.

It even smells of the Master's grace and greatness,
This message.

For this good news, I gave up my heart, but I was
Ashamed of the pauper's price which I was only able to pay.

It is thanks to God, and God alone, that his
Fee and my message cost the same.

What is the new physics of the orbiting planets and the revolutions of the Moon?
Both turn obediently to the Master's call.

If the wind of solar hurricanes should smash two worlds together,
Both mankind and daylight would rise up to heaven's land.

O morning breeze, be bifocals made of pearls. Made from earth's happy dust,
Taken from the road to where the Master lives.

May we always be at His threshold, our heads bent down in prayer;
And we'll see who ends up sleeping on the hand and chest of the Beloved.

If an enemy speaks out against Háfez, what is there to fear?
Thanks to God, unafraid I'll stand up to any foe and fight!

— *16* —

O wind, if you are traveling abroad to the land of my Beloved,
Bring back just a scent of musky air from His hair.

For that Great Soul, I'd gladly give up my life
If that were written in the letter He sent by return mail.

Wind, if you are not granted an audience with Him,
Then bring me dust from His doorway and stairs for my eyes.

I am nothing more than a lost gypsy. Where am I, lost and longing for Union?
If not in body, perhaps I will see my Beloved in sleep.

Although He wouldn't give a dime for us,
In exchange for the whole world we wouldn't trade even a hair from His head.

What is it worth if my heart were freed from the chains of grief and longing?
For Háfez would still be a slave. A servant forever of the one we call Friend.

— 17 —

Come here, for the House of Hope is built on quicksand;
Bring wine, for life's foundation is like the wind.

I am the slave of the One who is free of even
The color of attachment as it exists beneath the blue sky.

Let me tell you the good news that I heard last night
From the Angel of Beyond while lying drunk on the Winehouse floor!

"All you far-sighted royal falcons sitting in Paradise tree,
Don't nest in some dark corner of this sad land."

"From the highest hill in Heaven, fortress walls are calling you:
How have you and your kind fallen into such a trap?"

Listen to the advice I am about to give.
Think about it, and then act!

Don't expect this hysterical world to keep its promise;
This deceitful bride who has cheated on her wedding night with a thousand grooms."

Remember my advice. Don't serve your heart up on a platter for the world to eat.
Be content with what fate gives you, and don't frown.
The door of free choice for you and me is tightly bound.

There is no sign of faith or promise in the smile of the rose.
So weep, my loving nightingale, for this is Lamentation-Land.

You witless poets, why are you so envious of Háfez?
Sweet words that stir the heart and mind, are a gift from God!

— 18 —

With wine in hand and my Beloved, like a rose, inside,
Today the king of the world is my slave!

Please don't bring a candle when you come to our gathering tonight,
For tonight, we only want moonlight on the face of the Beloved.

We believe in the law of wine, it's true;
O Rose of the world, to be without Your face is wrong!

When You come to our gathering in Your name, You needn't wear rose perfume;
Our souls want only the musky smell of Your hair.

My ears are full of the sounds of clarinets and harps,
My eyes see only Your ruby lips circling the winecup of bliss.

Don't talk to me of the sweetness in sugar and candy,
For I am hungry only for the sweetness of Your kiss.

Since this treasure of grief for You has filled my ruined heart,
The corner of the Winehouse has become my home.

You ask me about shame? Shame gave me my name!
You want to know about fame? Fame is shame's mansion!

I am just a winedrinker—head spinning and looking for love.
In this city, is there anyone who is not like this?

Don't go and tell the priest of my shortcomings, for he, too,
Like me, is always looking for a jug of wine to get high.

Háfez, don't sit still even for a moment without the company of wine and
The Beloved. In this season of roses and jasmine, rejoice!

With cup in hand, the Beloved one day walked into the Winehouse.
And with only a wink, intoxicated all those already drunk with wine.

The hoofprint of Your horse looked like the shape of the new moon,
And Your shadow shrunk the size of the cypress pine to human scale.

Can I say truly: "I exist," when I don't know my true Self?
Can I truly say: "I don't," when I'm expecting The Divine?

When You got up to leave, the hearts of those in the Winehouse sank.
When You sat back down, the cheer that went up was deafening.

If any perfume smells like musk, it's because it was near Your hair.
If indigo is used to draw a fine blue rainbow, it was taken from the brow
of Your eyes.

My life is like a candle that has burned all night, and has burned away:
And like the burned moth, I will not rest until I see the light of day.

O Beloved, came back, so that Háfez's spent life will be returned to him;
Like an arrow, against all of nature, shot from his drunken bow.

— *20* —

O preacher, what is all this commotion? Go about your own work.
My heart fell from my hands long ago. What is wrong with your job?

The link between man and the Beloved, which God created from Nothing,
Is something that no high priest or scholar can explain.

The beggar in Winestreet is free of the eight houses of Paradise.
He that is bound and captive by You, is free from both worlds.

Even though I am drunk with love, and ruined:
I have grown healthy from drinking that wine.

O my heart, stop your complaining, you are not a battered spouse!
Your Lover has warned you again and again of this pain.

Like wind in my ear or like lips that caress the reed of a flute
If You are caressing my wish, I will not turn my back on the world.

Háfez, go, explain no more stories or recite more magical verse;
If they haven't gotten the message yet, don't waste your breath.
Turn your lips, instead, to the face of the Beloved!

— 21 —

Like blood dripping from the dew
I see You and surrender my soul. This is my only goal.

Those dark eyes and long eyelashes seduce whoever is touched by their glance.
You are the thief-of-hearts, but the blame is entirely mine.

Camel driver, don't carry my karma far from the gate;
This cul de sac is a royal highway, where my Beloved lives.

I am my own worst enemy in this age of adultery,
Yet the wine-drenched love I have for You, is my only affair.

He who carries the rose alongside the casket of ambergris
Smells nothing like the scent that comes from my Perfumer to this nose!

Gardener, don't chase me from Your garden like the wind.
These red, rare tears of mine are water for Your fruit.

O physician of this sick heart, prescribe doses of rosewater for me
From Your lips!

Whoever taught Háfez to write these poems, softly,
Has the voice of a nightingale in love, and is, for life, my friend.

It's been a long time since I've been out barhopping and chasing girls.
The thought of those days is a sad memory, yet some consolation.

In order to see God you've got to have eyes that can see the soul.
Where is the One who can see into the world in which I live?

Will You be my friend, whether for just one beautiful day or for all time?
Coming from Your face, tears look like the Pleiades in the night sky.

Since this gift of poetry I write truly came from Your love,
Everyone walks around now trying to rhyme with Your name.

O Lord, lock me safely into this house of poverty where I live.
Without this solitude and lack of wealth I couldn't even write a good line.

O preacher, errand boy of kings, give up on your crusade of pride,
For the Great King lives in a house of desperation, like mine.

O Lord, are You amused with my desire?
The domestic rose and the wild rose both live in thornbushes.

Who taught You to let Your imagination sail like the wind over water?
Perhaps it was guided by tears, that look like the Pleiades in the night sky.

Háfez, tell no more stories of the power of kings and easy saints,
Whose lips were merely drains for the sweet concoction I call wine!

It's true: for prayer, the Wineshop is the best monk's cell for me,
And praying at dawn to the Winemaker is true praise!

Don't worry about me, in my hands I have the sweet harp of a glass of wine,
My only excuse is my crying which you can hear at the crack of dawn.

Thank God, I have had enough of kings and beggars:
He who begs for dust from the Beloved's door, is king enough for me,

On my pilgrimage from mosque to Wineshop I only want to be with You.
As God is my witness, this is all I want!

I would rather, any day, be a beggar than a king.
True honor and true fame is found in submission.

Since the day that I set foot on Your high doorstep,
Somewhere in the bed of sun's heaven there's a pillow waiting for me.

It would be easy for me to fly off from this world.
But to sit outside Your door is my destiny.

Háfez, be a good boy and say this after me: "It's all my fault."
I know I have chosen this life, and that I have had no choice.

A thousand hearts have been captured by a single strand of hair,
Thousands, and no way out!

To tease the masses who would give up their soul for a sweet breeze,
You spray the odor of musk all around Your house, then shut the door
when they come sniffing by–

I became as mad as the moon when I saw the Beloved's face!

The Winebringer has poured into my cup, a wine of many colors.
In this one glass alone I can see the image of all creation.

O Lord, tell me how it is that wine sticks to the lip of the pitcher,
Like blood. And yet when it is poured a sweet glugging fills the air.

What melody was it the singer sang in the center of his song
That seems more like the truth than his words?

The Magician who knows that this world is just a trick of Illusion,
Has packed up all His equipment, and keeps quiet about the whole affair.

Háfez says: "Anyone who wants union but has never tried to love
Would probably, even with a dirty heart, wear the clothes of a pilgrim."

— 25 —

These days the only friend that is faultless
Is a bottle of red wine and a book of poems.

Wherever you are going, go alone, for the road to enlightenment is
Very narrow and full of curves.
And take your wineglass with you, for there are no guarantees.

I am not the only writer that is worried about having a job.
Knowledge without experience is the "wise man's" fate.

In this noisy street, the voice of reason says:
The world and all its possessions is no security.

Let me tell you an old story: The face of an old camel destined by
Fate to be black, cannot become white from washing and cleaning.

Everything you see around you, will one day disappear,
Except Love, which lasts forever.

I had great hopes that, with my heart, I would unite with You.
But along the road of Life, death lurks like highway robbery.

I say hold on to the moon-faced One's hair, and don't tell a soul!
For the effect of Saturn and the stars, is agony and good luck.

No one will ever see Háfez sober, never;
He is drunk on the wine of endless Eternity, and keeps asking for more!

— 26 —

If I have You in my mind, what use is wine?
Say to the winekeg: "Go away, I have decreed an end to all winehouses."

Even if you are serving your friends the wine of Paradise, pour it out:
For without the Beloved, each mouthful you give is only the essence
of torment and teasing.

Help! The Heartstealer has gone away. Through my weeping eyes
The idea of a letter from Him, is like reading words floating on the
water of a rushing stream.

Wake up! Open your eyes.
While you have been asleep, you have drifted into the rapids.

As the Beloved passes by in an open boat, all He sees are strangers,
And this is why He always wears a veil.

Since this rose first saw Your flushed cheek soaked in sweat,
It has been hot with greed, and dissolving in the salt-water of the heart's tears.

So don't go looking for advice in the corners of my brain,
They are filled with the hum of the harp and the flute.

The Path is a long road. Compared to its vastness,
The pounding ocean of the sky is only a mirage--a bubbling brook.

The valleys and the plains are green this time of year; so come, let's not
Waste our time looking for water, for the world is a mirage.

At the heart's banquet, a thousand candles are lit by Your face.
And for every candle there is a veil on Your face that is guaranteed.

O Candle that lights up my heart, with You
My heart is like roast meat, burnt and bleeding.

What does it matter if Háfez is a lover, a drunk, or a dancer?
As young pilgrims we have use for all of these.

— 27 —

Now that I have raised the glass of pure wine to my lips,
The nightingale starts to sing!

Go to the librarian and ask for the book of this bird's songs, and
Then go out into the desert. Do you really need college to read this book?

Break all your ties with people who profess to teach, and learn from the Pure Bird.
From Pole to Pole the news of those sitting in quiet solitude is spreading.

On the front page of the newspaper, the alcoholic Chancellor of the University
Said: "Wine is illegal. It's even worse than living off charity."

It's not important whether we drink Gallo or Mouton Cadet: drink up!
And be happy, for whatever our Winebringer brings, is the essence of grace.

The stories of the greed and fantasies of all the so-called "wise-ones,"
Remind me of the mat-weavers who tell tourists that each strand is a yarn of gold.

Háfez says, "the town's forger of false coins is also president of the city Bank.
So keep quiet, and hoard life's subtleties. A good wine is kept for drinking, never sold."

— 28 —

O hypocrite, you are so perfect, why do you criticize the lover of wine?
Don't worry, the sins of others won't count against you in the Good Deed
Book of God.

And don't worry about whether I'm "good" or "bad,"
In the end, we reap what we sow. So, go, take care of yourself.

Don't try and make me feel guilty or hopeless of ever attaining grace;
How do you know who is "saint" and who is "sinner," hiding there
behind that screen?

Everyone, sober or drunk, is in his own way, seeking the Beloved.
Whether mosque, church or a stand of trees, everywhere is a place of prayer.

I'm not the only one who has fallen from grace.
Even my father Adam was kicked out of the Eden of the Divine.

I lay my head, each night, in submission on the brick at the Winehouse door.
Critic, if you don't understand this, then you've nothing but bricks in your head.

It's true, that the garden of Paradise is beautiful. But be careful! And don't
Be deceived, for the shade of the willow and the edge of the woods are also great
treasures.

Do you really think you are the author of this book on which you have written
your name? Were you there on the day of Creation, when the pen of the Creator
wrote out your list of Fate?

If you understand what I am saying, then you are one of the bright ones, indeed!
And if this is your nature, then you should be proud!

O Háfez, if you die with a wine glass in your hands, from Winehouse Street
To the Governor's Estate, without casket, you will ride!

— 29 —

Even the rose smells the breath of the garden of Paradise.
And the wine of Joy and I are united in the eyes of the Beloved.

Today, why shouldn't the beggar boast of having his own kingdom,
With a feast-table the breadth of creation, and a roof of milky skies?

With the coming of spring, the Maker of Life tells us the one true story:
He who ignores today's beauty, is tomorrow's fool.

Fill my heart with the wine of Love 'til it overflows!
For this rotten world is nothing but dust. Everything dies.

One thing you can count on: the enemy is always unfaithful.
So don't waste your time trying to get even a spark from a monk's candle
that is lit by a church that is dead.

Don't criticize me for mistakes that I've made due to my ignorance!
Have you walked the path carved on my skull by the tides?

Don't walk away from the grave of Háfez,
Although he is buried in mistakes, he is traveling to Paradise!

— *30* —

O fanatic, don't invite me to Paradise and then turn around and walk away.
God didn't make me one of Paradise's people on that First Day.

You surround yourself with rosaries, prayer mats, austerity, chastity,
Prayer bells and a tiny room—The Master's pure wine's my way.

O sinless Sufi, who are you to tell me not to drink? For the All Wise
With pure wine, mixed and kneaded our clay.

A true Sufi isn't fit for Paradise if he hasn't, like me,
Given his coat of religion as payment for Winehouse wine.

Wise ones, do not reward a man with kisses
Who has given away the garment of the Beloved.

One cannot reap even one grain from the harvest of life
Unless on this path of illusion, he sows seeds on God's highway.

Háfez, if you want God's grace and generosity,
Give up Hell's troubles and Paradise's bliss; give them all away!

From the fire in my heart, my chest from grief for the Beloved, has burnt up.
And with it, now my whole house has burned down, too.

Because of separation from the Heartstealer, my body has melted
From the flames of love coming from His cheek.

Whoever has seen even the chain of curls framing the Beloved's face
Has had his desperate heart burnt up, like me.

Look at my heart. It's on fire from the heat of my tears.
Last night, as I watched a candle, a moth went up in flames!

It's not hard for me to believe that the hearts of my friends are on fire
For me. Since I've been in this state, even the hearts of strangers,
everywhere, are burning up.

This must be the Apocalypse! The Winehouse has flooded and caught on fire, too.
Now, my clothes of religious dogma and my house of reason are gone.

Because of all the promises I've made, the cup of my heart is broken.
And my liver, from all this good wine from the Winehouse, has gone up in flames.

Enough of all this nostalgia! It's enough to say that I've thrown off
This cloak of religion, and with a prayer, thrown it into the fire.

Háfez, give up all this small talk. You sound like an old woman afraid of death.
Drink some wine! All this chatter is only robbing us of sleep and a long life; and as a
breeze blows the flame of a candle quickly and burns
it up, our life is passing by…

Winebringer, come quick! For the Beloved has taken off His veil.
And the monks in the monastery have taken all the lamps.

How am I going to see His face with only this small candle?
By the time I get there He will be an old man!

A single glance from the Beloved, and all reverence was run off the road.
Enemies of beauty and virtue saw this and moved over into the fast lane!

Because of the birds of grief that had broken our hearts,
God sent us Christ to take up our travail.

O Beloved, now that you are here, under the sun and moon;
Work has taken a new meaning.

The radios of the seven heavens are playing this story over the air waves.
While those with small ears listen to stations only playing silly songs.

Háfez, where did you learn the magic of writing words?
The Beloved seems to have turned your weary wail into gold!

The Ocean of Love is a sea where there is no shore;
And without the soul's surrender, there is no hope, no sand.

When you come here on pilgrimage, don't bore us with
Your stories of judges and human laws; bring wine!

Another hour with your psychiatrist will not bring you bliss.
Instead, give your seconds and soul-money to Love and good deeds.

Don't blame your bad luck on the stars or the door of fate
That creaks, look in the mirror and ask your own eyes
who it is that wants you dead.

Like the crescent moon, the new moon's splendor in
Your new face can only be seen with pure eyes.

So go on — take up the goosechase of drunkenness;
And pretend you are looking for the buried treasure that will set you free.

If Háfez's tears do not move you,
then why has your heart not yet turned to stone?

— 34 —

No one has ever seen Your face, but still there are thousands of watchers
Waiting for the chance. Although you're still in bed, sleeping, nightingales
have been singing since dusk.

It's not so surprising that I have come to Your Street, at last.
Here in this country, we are all strangers.

O Great One, may no one be as far from you as I am.
But I am moving nearer... once was lost but now am found.

In the country of Love, the church and the tavern are the same.
Wherever they are, there Your light shines, too.

The prayers of the Christian monk are no different
From the sand swept by the rake of the one who follows Zen.

Show me even one lover whose pain the Beloved didn't see!
Sir, there is no such thing as pain. And if there were, the Physician
is there to prescribe the right wine.

When all is said and done, all of Háfez's crying was not for nothing.
As strange as his story may seem, it is a tale of great wonder, and true!

— 35 —

I want to tell You of my heart's desire.
And to hear the news of Your heart, too!

My wish is real simple, and a well known story:
To be anonymous and invisible to spies.

This precious holy "Night of Power" with you, is like a dream come true–
It has gone by so fast I have noticed only daylight.

In this dark night, I want to know every part of You.
To touch every tender part of You like a rare pearl.

O East Wind, help me through this night.
Help me to make it to morning so that I can bloom.

To prove to You my praise is worthy, I would
Sweep the dust from the Path with my eyelashes.

Háfez pays no attention to the censors and the critics;
Writing poems full of love, beyond reason, is his one desire.

— *36* —

O You, Who have disappeared, I am giving You to God.
You burned my soul, yet I still hold You in my heart.

As long as the hem of my pants is dragging above ground,
I will attach myself, like lint, to what You wear.

Even the altar of Your eyebrows in the morning
Is enough to make me raise my hands in prayer!

If need be, I'll go all the way to Babylon
To learn enough sorcery to make You mine.

Rather, through an act of grace, let me come to You with my heart on fire
And pearls raining from my eyes to bathe Your feet.

Over my chest a hundred streams are flooding from these eyes
Wanting to sow just one loveseed in the bed of Your garden soil.

By spilling my blood You've freed me from separation's grief.
And for this wound Your knife-sharp glance has opened in my ribs, I thank You!

O Great Doctor, all I want is to die at Your feet.
I've been sitting in this Waiting Room of life, now, too long.

And if, in waiting, my eye and heart should stray and want another;
I promise to set fire to my heart and cut out my eyes for forsaking You.

Háfez: sex, wine, and drunken women are not the Beloved's style.
Since you have waited like this so long, the Doctor is going to see you now,
for free.

Thank God that the Winehouse is open!
For forever on that door is where I want my face.

Inside, the wine barrels are drunk and brawling:
"Truth!" they shout, and they do not lie.

The Beloved is amused with our rowdiness and pride.
We, in our drunkenness, are proud of our helpless begging.

The secret I haven't told the masses and will never tell,
I will tell to the Beloved, who already knows.

Strands of hair, curls within curls, all have an explanation which can
Never be shortened by the hairdresser, and looks long from any side.

Háfez's heavy heart has more curls than Layla's hair.
To the cheek of Mohammad the foot of the Buddha is tied.

Tired of being witness to the world, I've sewn up my eyes;
And like the devoted falcon I sit perched on Your cheek.

He who enters Winestreet also enters the Winehouse
Through the arch of Your eyes, and is destined to become drunk with prayer.

O friends, ask me about the fire in my heart.
It is a candle that has burned so long that now it is only tears.

— 38 —

O Lord, I'm still drunk from the smell of Your fragrant hair.
Every minute is consumed by the sorcery of Your blinding stare.

After such long patience, will we ever see a night when we will
Light the candles of our eyes in Your eyebrow's altar of prayer?

This blackboard in my eyes is sacred. On it are drawings of the soul.
And a perfect likeness of Your dark face.

O Lord, if You really want to make this world beautiful,
Tell the breeze to lift the veil off Your fair face.

Or if You want to merely rid the world of all its waste and trash:
Just shake Your head and let thousands of souls fall from every hair.

I have the kindness of the breeze to thank for the perfume of the Beloved.
Here in the morning's dawn, it's all I've got.

I always knew that black center in the eye sought my heart's blood.
I have made it sacred, for it reminds me of Your mole.

Hooray for Háfez's good humor! In both this world and the next,
Nothing gets in his eye but dust from the end of the Road.

The value of all the gold in the world is worthless: Nothing.
Winebringer, bring wine! Because this whole world and its business
is nothing, too.

Both heart and soul of Háfez desire the Beloved's presence.
To him this is Everything! And without that, life and happiness is nothing.

Good luck comes to the heart, painless and without blood.
Food picked in the Garden of Paradise gained by blood and stress is not
real food.

If you are tired and hot, don't go looking for shade beneath the Tree of
Life, or beneath the lotus! There is no cool breeze unless you know the Truth.

Life on this earth is short, and is gone, like a short work-week.
Use this time to rest, for even this time does not exist.

O Winebringer, we are merely waiting on the shore of the ocean of death.
Fill our cups while you can. Even the time it takes to drink a sip of wine
is gone too fast.

Friends, don't worry about what people say, be the happy rose,
The power of this passing world is like the breeze--gone. And is nothing.

And I say to the professors: be careful, and don't always think you are right.
For the distance from the monk's cell to the Master's abode, is less than
you think.

I have been worn away to nothing from all this grief and suffering.
Yet, there's no need for me to confess to any priest, for this, too,
is nothing.

"Háfez" is a name that has the seal of approval;
But the wino is not impressed: to have much or to have nothing is both the
same, and is Nothing.

Because the Perfect Master stands here before my eyes, Life is a joy!
In the Winehouse garden, the weather is also perfect.

It's good that those with generous hearts lay their heads at His feet.
To explain this shows lack of respect and is unfair.

The story of Paradise and its heavenly House
Is merely a symbol explaining the grave of the grapevine's daughter, and is rare.

While the miser digs forever for his silver and his gold,
The Spirit of our heart is searching for the cup of red wine.

In all Eternity, and before there was Time, on everyone's head was written:
"This is the house of idols and jails; welcome to Hell and Paradise."

The truth is: No treasure can be bought without consulting, first, the snake.

The jewel of Pure Essence is a true prize, so work to do good.
There is no loss of honor in being born to wealth or impressive bloodlines.

By this same Path, the heart of Háfez is working hard.
Striving day and night, searching forever for the grace of God.

— *41* —

The fasting is over, the feast has begun, and hearts full of joy are awake!
In the Winehouse, the wine is flowing…. Drink up!

The hour of bragging by the sober ones is over, and life's heaviness is gone.
It is time now for joyful drinkers to happily indulge!

Why should we be condemned for drinking such fine wine?
For the drunken lover, this habit is neither a crime nor a mistake.

The wino who is not a hypocrite or full of deceit,
Is better than a pious braggart with hypocrisy written all over his face.

Here in the Winehouse, we are not hypocrites, drunk on deceit.
He Who knows our hearts will attest to this in a court of law.

We carry out the commandments of God and don't hurt anyone.
And whatever we are told is "unlawful," we don't twist to make it "law."

What do you care if I drink a few cups of wine?
They're not using your blood to make this drink from the blood of the vine!

This weakness of mine will hurt no one.
And if it were a "sin," so what? Show me a man who has never made a mistake!

Háfez, stop all this chatter of "How and Why," and drink some wine!
What good is this talking of "laws" when, with your lips, of the Divine Order
you do partake.

— 42 —

Upon hearing the Master's words, don't say: "This is wrong."
My friend, it is you that are mistaken and have the wrong idea.

I do not bow down to this mad world or any other;
Instead, I praise God, for because of Him, I have become God-mad!

I'm not really sure who it is inside my broken heart,
For I am silent and shy, and it rants and raves all day!

O Minstrel, I have run out of patience;
Come quick, and sing songs to me that will lighten this load.

I have never paid much attention to the work of this weary world,
For in Your Face I have seen the world for the illusion it really is.

Because I imagined I was mature and wise, I gave up sleeping.
But after a hundred hangovers, I still make my way, each night, to the
Winehouse for more wine.

Now, my livingroom is full of blood from my bleeding heart.
And I spend all day trying to clean the carpet with wine.

What was the tune that the Minstrel played for me last night on Winestreet?
Even though life may have passed me by, I can't get it out of my head!

O Beloved, my love for You is so real!
It is a voice that fills my heart and speaks to me all day.

Ever since the moment that the Beloved's words entered his ears,
Háfez has become a mountain, from which that song's echo rings!

— *43* —

Help! Is there no remedy for this pain?
No pill that will make this separation go away?

Help! They've stolen my heart and all its love,
And now they want my soul!

Help! These heartstealers have no pity;
They have filed suit against soul as payment for a kiss.

These heartless bastards are drinking our blood;
O friends of God, Help!

Give help to the wretched:
Help them through these long and deadly nights.

Look inside our hearts, and see! Just when we think that the old pain is
Gone, there is new pain to take its place.

Help! I have watched Háfez for years with his weeping.
He is on fire. And now I think it's me!

— 44 —

Like the wind, I'll make my way to the end of the Beloved's street.
I'll make my breath into rain-musk from His sweet perfume.

All the water that I've gathered from His face from faith and knowledge,
I'll scatter on the path to the Beloved's feet to settle the dust.

Except for wine and the Beloved, my life has been a waste.
From now on, I promise to make idleness a spiritual retreat.

Where's that wind? I am ready to sacrifice my bloody life
For the sweet perfume of the Beloved's hair.

Let me say it again: Like a lit candle in the darkness of morning shows its
Love for the light, my gift to the Beloved is my life.

So strong is the Ancient Promise in me, that I am going to make myself mad;
And when they ask, I will only remember His name.

Háfez says, "Hypocrisy and disagreement won't purify your heart.
My path is that of drunkenness and my street is the Street of Love."

To worry even for a moment about all of creation is worthless.
Sell it all for wine, because our need for religion is worthless, too.

In Winemakers Street they don't give you a cup for seriousness.
What use is a prayer mat to a worthless drunk!

Wash out the color of this many-colored coat of deceit and illusion;
The true color of red wine and the coat is black.

To risk one's life for pride and the seductive crown of majesty
Is a waste of time.

When I went on an ocean voyage looking for lost treasure,
I was wrong dreaming about a hundred pearls.

Don't worry. Be happy! With what you have this moment.
The treasures of the heart are not found on land or at sea.

The Beloved's wish is our only purpose and home.
Being anywhere other than where He is, is being lost.

Like Háfez, don't worry. Let go of the selfish world
That clings to you like a ton of miser's gold.

At the gate of the marketplace, the soul-gamblers shout:
"Hear this, you who dwell in 'God's country', for 'God's sake'!"

It's been weeks now, since the beautiful daughter of wine disappeared,
Following the lusty path of her own bliss and on the make!

Dressed in rags of rubies and a water crown,
She steals the minds and hearts of the unsuspecting.
Beware. Don't sleep. Stay wide awake!

To whomever brings her to me, I'll give him my soul like gold.
And if she is hiding in Hell, then take me there so I can see.

Even though she prowls the drunken night with rosy thorns,
Háfez says, "If you find her, bring her home to me!"

Happiness is: a river's bank, the shade of a willow, and the poetic mind of a friend.
Happiness is: The Winebringer with rosy red cheeks who has stolen my heart.

Hey, what good luck that my destiny should have no idea of time.
May it continue!

To anyone whose heart knows friendship from loving one Who would steal his
Heart, say: "Throw rice into the fire!" Who could have a better job than this?

To the bride-of-nature I give all my fantasies of virgins at night in my bed.
Perhaps the God of Time will someday send me a painting of a beautiful nude.

Know that even one night spent with the Beloved is a great gift.
Be happy, for the moon is shining, your heart's on fire, and the river is
low in its banks.

Look! There is wine in the glass eye of the Winebringer
That intoxicates reason and leaves you with a hangover of happiness!

Háfez, your life is slipping by: come with us to the Winehouse.
Don't feel guilty because you are homeless and out of work.
Be happy! The Perfect One is there paying off the bills of His lovers–With jobs and
offering a handsome wage.

Come closer, so I can trace the smell of my soul from Your cheek,
Where I have found footprints of my former heart.

All the spells and epiphanies we've read of in books
Are explained in the beauty and grace of Your cheek.

The body of the proud cypress becomes dust in the shadow of that shape:
Where even the rosegarden rose shyly shrinks from that face.

Like rosewater brought up from the well of the jawbone,
The perfume of the Beloved that is drawn up as a muskpod of China
takes the fragrance of musk from Your hair.

The sun is drowned in the rainsweat from the Sun of Your eyes:
Leaving only a thin waning moon in the sky –

The Water-of-Life is flowing down from Háfez's poems
Dissolving souls into sweat that fall like lace from His skin.

— 49 —

Ever since softening the Beloved's cheek with down, Time drew the line,
And the sky's moon mistook Your face as another moon's shine.

From wanting Your lip, which is far better than the Water of Life,
The fountain of water flowing from my eyes and the Euphrates are
a single stream.

Look at the gray-colored mole resting on that silver cheek;
Truly, all that remains of the moon's face now is the odor of musk!

Since You showed up in the garden covered in sweat and wild hair,
The face of the red rose has turned to saffron. Wet-hot and dripping with musk.

Sometimes I long for You so, I give away heart and soul like they were dust.
Sometimes like ducks, I quench this love's fire with the water of my own tears.

I will sign any contract that would bind me as a slave
To the Great King, if He would find me worthy!

O Háfez, the Water-of-Life is full of mud because of your poems:
No one has ever written words like this out of the desire for Love!

— *50* —

Friend, get up! You're blocking the door of the Winehouse.
Do you think you'll find meaning sitting there like that in the path
of the Beloved?

We don't have enough food for the long journey to the Beloved's house.
Let's go beg at the Winehouse door and then go on the road.

O Pure One, our tears are stained with blood,
And from our faces run down the road to You.

This grief tastes so sweet! O please take back this candy You send us.
Such hope is bad for our health.

Instead, send us the scent of Your hair's perfume.
A fragrant pill is all this sick heart needs.

The truth is: there is no grief except in a joyous heart.
I know, for on this journey, we have asked many questions, and opened
many doors.

Háfez says, "How long will you sit there in the door of the college?
Get up! You must be dreaming. This is not the Winehouse door!"

— 51 —

In the house of God, I can see God's Light clearly.
I must remember to write down where and what I see.

O Lord, I wonder who it is that drinks all the dregs in the Winehouse.
His door is a prayer arch for prayer and a touchstone for all need.

Everything I need is in this Winehouse.
My life as lover, drunkard and a man in love, is good.

O pied piper of pilgrims, don't boast to me of your fame.
You see only the house, but it is He Who owns the house I see!

From as far away as China or Tibet, no one has seen
What I see at dawn from musk-scented zephyrs from the East.

In the circle of all creation, except for the point of Unification,
There is nothing. Why ask "how" and "why" of things if this is true?

From the long flowing hair of worldly beauties, I will steal the musk.
Is this a "mustake" to love this smell?

My heart is on fire, my tears are streaming, and I weep nightly and sigh
At dawn. All because my life is tied up in a sweet scent that can't be seen.

Suddenly, my thoughts have been ambushed by the apparition of Your face!
Who can I tell, now that I can see again through this veil of ignorance?

Friends, do not think less of Háfez for looking lustfully at beautiful women.
I love you too. When I look at women this way, I see only lovers of God.

Last night in desperation, I screamed: "Rid me of this longing for Your face!"
You responded by tying me to the doorway in chains.

I begged for Your forgiveness, and in anger You turned away–
O friends, now what will I do? My Lover's upset and won't face the truth.

O Heartstealer, I am sorry for what I said;
Be benevolent so that at least I can continue to write.

This separation has turned my face yellow with pain.
O Winebringer, give me some wine, to bring back the color of roses to my face.

O Wind from the house of Layla, my tears have flooded one fourth of the world.
How long can this storm go on?

Since I have taken the path of devotion to the Beloved,
I have the power to make a hundred beggars rich, and a pauper of the king.

O Moon-of-Faithfulness, don't forget to remember Your slave Háfez.
I pray every day to Your beauty, and I am filled with grace!

— 53 —

I've done hard-labor for years in the Winehouse.
But dressed in beggar's rags, I count myself among the blessed!

The critic hasn't a clue to what's going on. To his face I say:
"Stop your backbiting and you will begin to be wise."

Until I can bring that strutting ostrich into the trap of union,
He will always be looking over his shoulder for a pointed gun.

The Heart rises and falls like the breeze walking down Winestreet.
And I pray for help, with basil and roses, with each step.

The Heartstealer's hair is the trap, and His glance the arrow:
O heart, your career is moving slowly, where will you go now for free advice?

O Beloved, there is already too much dust in Your street!
I am disappearing, like a whirlwind, in all that dust.

O Merciful One, cover the eyes of those that only see my life of seclusion
And devotion as a great mistake.

God forbid that I should not cower with fear from "Resurrection Day"!
I get all my prophecy from today's good cheer.

From the right hand of God, deceitful deniers shout, "Amen!"
Meanwhile, I pray that my Lord of mountains and streams does hear.

O Beloved, I only want to see the mountaintop.
To stand in prayer there, and to kiss the sky!

Look at me! I'm Háfez at the religious gathering, drinking the dregs with
My friends. This is a career move for me, this humble drinking.
And I've done it with bold joy and ease!

I'm embarrassed to come before You
With arms that are too short and my heart a wreck.

If only these short arms could reach those long curls.
Without that soft embrace I will surely go mad.

Just ask my eyes about the patterns of planets:
I don't sleep. I count stars all night until dawn.

Like magic, after kissing the lips of the Great Cup,
The secrets of Time and Space were revealed!

Thank God I'm not a man of strength, this is good luck;
For I don't want to even harm a hair on the head of the human race,

Today, I make a prayer for all the Winesellers. And why shouldn't I?
To return the kindness and free drinks of such a generous host.

Yet, with all this prayer, you could not raise me from the dead, or from
The dust of sorrow. My eyes are pouring pearls where tears used to be.

Don't pity me for drinking the blood of my own grief.
For my teacher and guardian is a deer invisible to arrows of the one who
hunts for meat.

In the Winehouse of Love is where you'll find me, drinking
All night these musky dregs, and making no sense.

Even though Háfez is dead drunk and half crazy,
His face is lit up and his body alive with the hope and grace of the Beloved!

— 55 —

O Beloved, don't give Your hair to the breeze, or the wind will be the death
Of me. If You give foundation to contempt, You'll knock me off my feet.

Free me from the roseleaf through the light in Your face.
Show me Your body, so I can be free of this love of leaves.

If You become well-known in the city, I will have to retreat to the hills.
If You drink wine with others, I'll have to start drinking my own blood.
Don't think of those barroom friends; remember me!

Twisting Your hair into curls is like putting me in jail.
The beauty of Your face is already more than I can take.

If You are too friendly with strangers, I will become jealous.
Don't even think of them when they are gone, for You have me.

Because You are the candle of every gathering, it is me that is consumed
By light. Don't look away. I can't bear the absence of Your stare.

O Beloved, have pity on me, and hear my complaints.
Please, I am not just the dust of the door, complaining.

If Your Love is like the thunder and lighting in the sky, it will kill
Háfez. Be gentle, I am a frail servant who only wants to love his life,
and live!

— *56* —

Today is the birthday of the new moon, and instead of
Fasting for thirty days I'm going to drink all day.

It's been a long time since I've been separated from wine and wineglass,
And I'm beginning to feel ashamed by this affair.

To set a good example, from now on I'll not sit in seclusion
Even if the religious fanatic of the cloister chains up my legs to make me stay.

Even the city's most prestigious preacher is giving me his saintly advice,
But I am not listening to anyone, now or in ten thousand days.

Where is even one man who gave up his life to the dust on the Winehouse door?
It is on his foot that I want to lay my head and die.

Meanwhile, I keep on drinking wine, draped in the robes of reverence.
God help me if the news of my double life should reach the ears of gossips!

Those that live along the grapevine say: "O Háfez, listen to the words of the
Wise old man." I have tried, but old wine means more to me than a hundred
old men today.

I am in love with a youthful and joyous face!
And I have prayed to God that from my state of grief, I might embrace joy.

I will say it for all the world to hear: I am drunk and looking for love!
I'm not just a wino down on his luck.

In fact, I'm even embarrassed for my ragged coat stained with wine,
And its patches that cover up all of my lies.

O little candle, how happy you look burning down in desire for the One you
Love. But look, I am also in this business, all belted and ready and standing
in line!

All the money I've made from working in the Wineseller's box,
And all I've got to show for that work is half a heart and soul.

All night long I stand guard at the stonehenge of my heart.
Maybe the full moon will move a little closer so that I can see His face.

I think I will go to the Winehouse like Háfez, wearing his clothes,
So that when the Beloved Heartstealer comes, it is me instead of Háfez
He will embrace.

— *58* —

My grief is so strong, that I don't even see a hint of the end of time.
There is no medicine or miracle cure for this depression, except wine.

No, I won't ignore the advice of the old Wineseller,
It's all I've got.

Even though I'm sick for wine, no one will give me a drink.
Is there no one left in the world with a compassionate heart?

As far as I can see, the essence of all life comes from the sun of the
Winecup. I am a direct descendant of that light, yet I am still in line for
the crown of Time.

The only way to be pure of heart is by being a lover.
The preachers and priests don't have a clue.

How I wish that my eyes weren't so blinded by weeping.
With these wet mirrors of mine, how can I see Your face?

All I can see now in these rivers I used to call eyes
Is more water and the memory of Your form.

In this swollen river, I clutch the boat of Háfez's *Divan*.
All I've got now to keep me afloat are words.

— 59 —

When slanderers criticize me, I remember:
It wasn't I who invented love and wine!

What right does someone as notorious as me have to
Tell the wino to stop drinking wine?

Just call me: "King of the Drunks," for I've lost my mind
To this wine, and am beyond saving, in this world or the next.

On my forehead, with my heart's blood, make Your mark,
So everyone can see and will know I'm beyond religion and have
given up to Fate.

So, winedrinker, go your own way, don't look to me for help.
If you look closely in this dervish's coat, you'd only see more wine.

O wind, send these lines raining heart's blood to my Friend.
The same Friend who got to the vein of my soul by shooting me up with pain.

Winebringer, stay clear of this bleeding heart,
This wound that loves wine is contagious!

Whether I'm a drunk or a Perfect Master, what do you care?
My secret is that I am only Háfez. He who writes poetry must
also love his wine!

What I will say to you, I say openly and with great joy:
I am the slave of Love, and from both worlds I have been freed!

O, the stories I could tell–how I fell into the trap of separation
But became the rose that lies in the Beloved's bed.

I was once an angel, my home was on Paradise Street.
But Adam lured me down here into this one-roomed cell with barely a bed.

Living here in Wineseller's Street
Has caused me to forget all about my hardships.

On the blackboard of the heart, I have straight A's in my love for the Beloved.
What else can I do? My Master only taught me one letter of the
alphabet, and that letter was an "A."

I've never been to an astrologer to tell me about my life.
O God, where on this Earth do I fit in?

Ever since I became the ear-ringed slave that you see
Standing at Love's Winehouse door, at least one new sorrow comes in every
minute and I am greeted by that sorrow.

Meanwhile, my eyes pour out the blood of my heart.
Why did I do it: give away my heart to someone else?

O Beloved, with the tips of Your curls, wipe these tears from Háfez's face.
Or mankind will experience another apocalypse in the form of the Flood.

You have been ignoring, for too long, your old friends.
Come here, and give me all your spite!

Listen to what my pen has to say: for this drop of ink
Is worth more than all the shining jewels you own.

If any of last night's wine is left,
Come to the cry of the intoxicated, sick for more wine.

But how can you show your face to those who make love to wine,
If the mirror of the sun and moon is too high for your eyes?

O wise one, be reasonable, don't speak out against love,
Unless it is with the love of God you have a quarrel.

Don't you fear my burning sigh at all!
You, there in your coat of flammable wool.

Háfez, I've never seen or heard poems more beautiful than yours,
Which, like the Koran, you hold tight and close to your heart.

— *62* —

Bartender! Bring me more wine! And take this hangover away.
With more wine, the suffering from wine disappears.

Except for on the face of an idol and the winegrape,
The lamp of a friendly gathering doesn't shine a single ray.

Don't take pride in the magic of your seductive glance!
For I've proven time and time again that pride doesn't pay.

Professor, you give such strange advice, from your books that say:
"Don't try love." I say: there is no expert in the name of Love.

The soul of the man with a heart is alive with love!
If you don't have love, you're excused from this class–now go away!

By being deceitful only once, I have given away my integrity.
And I cried for it all day.

But pain and separation passed, and good fortune came.
And my empty heart became prosperous and rich with love again to lose.

Háfez, you cannot tell everyone the secret of the heart so they'll understand;
But tell those who have suffered distance from the Beloved,
they will understand your song!

What if the beggar had been truly pure in his begging,
Would his empty cup have been heaped full of gold?

What if the sun had not been made from the stars,
Wouldn't his golden bowl then have been filled with good wine?

What if the mansions of the world were not destined, over time, to fall down,
Wouldn't their foundations be stronger and their roofs more resistant to rain?

What if man had not become slave to the mixing of metals, and
Left work in the Master's hands; who knows how this life, now, would be?

Look to the Beloved in this Age of confusion.
He alone can hear you, and make hands on the clock of Time stand still!

— *64* —

O secretary, schedule me some time to speak to the Master,
In a private place absent of even the breeze.

I'll show Him my wit and humor and make Him laugh.
And thus soften up His heart.

Heart softened, He will ask with generosity:
"Won't you come see me again next week, for on a weekly course should we be."

— *65* —

Why do you want to know if you are good or bad?
Have you forgot? Do you need another Judge?

Listen to what Háfez says: Stay away from the bad and work toward the good.
Do not play games or toy with life or it will rot.

Since you already know that God will provide for your needs:
Lighten up! Untie that knot in your heart and get rid of the greed.

Surrender yourself to the Beloved! Don't sit around waiting for help.
Surrender is like a loud voice that the Winebringer hears over all his other customers.
And He will bring you all the wine you need.

— 66 —

From the Book of Morals, let me read you
What it says about faith and generosity:

"If, from hate, your friend cuts you with his knife;
Like the bountiful mine, give him gold.

"Be like the tree, where they go in search of shade:
And instead of shade, drop fruit upon the stonethrowers.

"To anyone who tries to bite your head off with sharp tongue and teeth,
Give him a pearl. And tell him the story of how the oyster lives humbly
beneath the Sea.

— 67 —

O rich man, I have come from Paradise to bring you some happy news!

Amidst my sweet songs, my raucous jokes, and my beautiful stories
That will soothe your heart, there is also the truth.

I say, "This mansion is really a dwelling for the poor.
Put on a feast that costs you everything you have, in honor of
the real King of Wealth. And give it all away!"

— *68* —

How long must I sit here in the corner of this dark home waiting for God?
Biting my fingers, head on my knees, grieving...

I gave up patience when, like a wolf, I got cornered in a lion's den.
I gave up reason when, in the dove's nest, a crow began to sing.

O blessed Bird, come again and sing to me of better days;
Of the past, and of the future to which we will return.

— *69* —

O Winebringer, fill this cup; for this Master of the feast
Is granting wishes to all those who have been patient and asked for nothing.

He says: "O friends, you are living in the Garden of Eden, so have fun!"
God is not keeping score of every misdeed you have done.

Here in this dancehall of grasses and trees, the harp is singing.
Here, the Beloved's mole is heartbait, the Winebringer's hair the trap.

Friends, try and be friendly.
You may never be here again.

O Winebringer, there will never be a better day for happiness.
O Háfez, have another glass of wine! Today is all the time you need.

— *70* —

O mighty ruler, wake up! The army of God's Grace is at your door.
Last night you made plans to conquer the world. What will you do now?

From the height of glory, He knows where you began;
And of the plan He has for you for doing good in this life.

Aside from the magic of this rusty blue sword at your side,
What do you really have that is yours?

Háfez says, "Listen to my advice: This is your chance!
He who exchanges ten dollars for seven and a half, has made no profit.
But changing seven and a half into ten will make you Rich!"

The beauty of this poem is beyond words.
Do you need a guide to experience the heat of the sun?

Blessed is the brush of the painter who paints
Such beautiful pictures for his virgin bride.

Look at this beauty. There is no reason for what you see.
Experience its grace. Even in nature there is nothing so fine.

Either this poem is a miracle, or some sort of magic trick,
Guided either by Gabriel or the Invisible Voice, inside.

No one, not even Háfez, can describe, with words, The Great Mystery.
No one knows in which shell the priceless pearl does hide.

This morning, because of all my grief, while writing poetry,
My words revolted and ran away...

They ran, complaining, past the shrines of Rumi and Kabir,
And through the land of Solomon, and kept going...

They ran along the banks of the sacred river,
And by the palace of the king, and kept on going...

They ran past the house of the One who, alone,
Understands the soul of language, and kept on going...

I called out to my soul: "Old friend, where are you going?"
Its heartsick and weeping reply was angry and harsh, and it kept on going...

I shouted louder: "O words, will you never speak to me again in sweet rhymes?"
But the sweet words and the sweet verses only ran faster, kept going...

I pleaded: "Do not go!" But they turned a deaf ear,
Like that of the king or the chancellor who is too busy to be bothered with
the lovers of wine.

O Perfect Master, please call back these words of mine that have gotten away.
What is a man like Háfez, on fire, to do? Who with love overflowing, and
no words, has nothing more to say.

The blind and the deaf do not see or hear the resentment of the sky.

There are millions who have their heads in the clouds
Who will end up, like everyone else, with pillows of dust in a grave.

What kind of armour can you use against the arrows of destiny?
Can you stop Fate with a spear or a shield?

Even if you build walls around you out of iron and steel,
Death knocks down those doors when your time has come.

Don't feel so proud of "the good life," with its drink and sensuous desires.
Remember: darkness follows light. And there is poison in sugar,
just hiding there in its guise of sweetness as a snare.

If someone opens the door of desire for you, don't go through.
If someone offers to show you the path of lust, just walk away.

Know that in your path is a pit, so don't walk forward with a bowed head.
Know that in your wine cup there is also poison, so don't bring me your
untasted wine.

Háfez says, "Look into the dust of the crystal ball and see the nature of time.
Now, fold up your carpets of desire and tear in two your pages of
indulgent poems, and follow the Path that to the Beloved, comes.
This is the road that leads to the Winehouse.
It is for those seeking and those listening, not the blind, deaf, and dumb."

When will I ever find a little time so I may serve the Perfect Master?
And from the Master's advice, make my life young again.

For many years now, I have been caretaker of the Winehouse.
And have resigned myself to that job for the rest of my life.

Yesterday, the priest caught me with a bottle of wine, took it from me,
And threw it away ——
From now on I'll be careful, and carry my wine beneath my coat.

THOMAS RAIN CROWE is a poet, translator, essayist, editor and author of six books of original poetry, including his *Night Sun* trilogy published in 1993. As a translator he has translated the work of Yvan Goll, Hughes-Alain Dal, Guillevic, Marc Ichall and now Háfez. He is former editor of *Beatitude Magazine* and Beatitude Press (San Francisco), *Katuah Journal* (North Carolina), and is currently International Editor-at-Large for the *Asheville Poetry Review*. He is the founding publisher-producer of New Native Press and its subsidiary spoken-word & music recording label Fern Hill Records. He lives in Tuckaseegee, North Carolina with keyboardist-composer and translator Nan Watkins.